You'll Never Walk *Alone*

Publications International, Ltd.

Let's get social!

 @Publications_International

@PublicationsInternational

www.pilbooks.com

Table of Contents

Walking with God

We often think of life in terms of a journey—a walk through time in which we experience joy and sorrow, pleasure and pain, peace and turmoil. In the course of a lifetime, as we continue along—daily, weekly, monthly, yearly—upon the unique terrain of our own landscape, it can sometimes seem as though we are traveling alone.

The stories, prayers, and Bible verses included in this book are accounts of such times in the lives of people who have walked through difficulties. For many, it seemed as though they would become hopelessly stranded in their personal desert with no one to come alongside them with help. Yet in each, there was a wonderful discovery: At no time were they ever walking alone!

You may be experiencing your own trek through a desert place in life. It may feel as if the sun is scorching your mind and heart, the sand is blinding your spiritual eyes, your faith is dangerously low, and you do not have a sense of direction or even of hope. Worst of all, you might be feeling all alone with no one to hear you call for help. You need to know that you are not alone. God is there with you, and he will see you through your desert experience.

Throughout this book, you'll find inspiring quotes, reflections, verses, and prayers on every day of the calendar year to remind you that God is always with you. He will never abandon you in your desert. So take heart today! God sees you, he cares about you, he is with you, and he will help you. With him by your side, you will never walk alone.

January

January 1

And they heard the voice of the Lord God
walking in the garden in the cool of the day:
and Adam and his wife hid themselves from the
presence of the Lord God amongst the trees of
the garden.

—Genesis 3:8

Lord, when I feel like I am walking alone, it is often because I am walking away from you, or trying to hide from
you. In this coming year, let me always walk towards you,
refraining from sin and repenting from it.

January 2

Lord, this year I want for my faith to grow and deepen. I ask that you walk beside me and guide my steps as I read your Word, sit in silent prayer, and worship with others. Wherever my spiritual life seems frozen and desolate like the winter landscape, I ask you to bring it warmth and life and renewal. I ask you to send your Holy Spirit to rekindle my desire to love and serve you.

January 3

And the peace of God, which passeth all understanding, shall keep your hearts and minds through Christ Jesus.

—Philippians 4:7

Hopeful people have a peace about them, a way of looking at everything that happens as an opportunity for growth and happiness. Their lives are not any easier than anyone else's; it's their attitude that sets them apart.

January 4

To find love, we think we must first find the courage to take a big chance by risking our heart to another; yet it's only then that we discover it's in the very act of offering ourselves that love is found.

January 5

Peace I leave with you, my peace I give unto you: not as the world giveth, give I unto you. Let not your heart be troubled, neither let it be afraid.

—John 14:27

All around, the storms may churn,

the seas may rage, the fires burn.

But deep within you, you will not fear,

you will have peace when centered there.

For even amidst the tempest wild,

God will be there to guide you, child.

January 6

My Creator, blessed is your presence. For you and you alone give me power to walk through dark valleys into the light again. You and you alone give me hope when there seems no end to my suffering. You and you alone give me peace when the noise of my life overwhelms me. I ask that you give this same power, hope, and peace to all who know discouragement, that they, too, may be emboldened and renewed by your everlasting love. Amen.

January 7

Deep peace of the running waves to you.

Deep peace of the flowing air to you.

Deep peace of the smiling stars to you.

Deep peace of the quiet earth to you.

Deep peace of the watching shepherds to you.

Deep peace of the Son of Peace to you.

—Gaelic Prayer

The Lord will bless his people with peace.

—Psalm 29:11

In hope that sends a shining ray

far down the future's broad'ning way,

in peace that only thou canst give,

with thee, O Master, let me live.

—Washington Gladden,
"O Master, Let Me Walk With Thee"

January 9

I will instruct thee and teach thee in the way
which thou shalt go: I will guide thee with
mine eye.

—Psalm 32:8

Ah, what solace there is in your promise of peace. True
help and real peace are to be found from trusting in your
guidance, your teaching, and your inspiration.

January 10

Dear God, your love embraces me like the warmth of the sun, and I am filled with light. Your hope enfolds me in arms so strong, I lack for nothing. Your grace fills me with the strength I need to move through this day. For these gifts you give me, of eternal love, eternal peace, and most of all, for eternal friendship, I thank you God.

January 11

The Lord bless thee, and keep thee:
The Lord make his face shine upon thee, and be
gracious unto thee:
The Lord lift up his countenance upon thee,
and give thee peace.

—Numbers 6:24–26

Lord, bring me to the place where peace flows like a river, where soft green grasses gently hold the weight of my tired body, where the light of a new sunrise casts warmth.

January 12

Lord, dismiss us with thy blessing,

Hope, and comfort from above;

Let us each, thy peace possessing,

Triumph in redeeming love.

—Robert Hawker

January 13

Your faithful companionship is what is consoling me right now, O God. Sometimes my family and friends don't feel comfortable around my grief. Maybe they're afraid of saying or doing the wrong thing. I can understand that, and I know that they still care. But thank you, dear Lord, for not staying away. You wait in silence with me, and you speak truth and love to me when I need it most. My faith in you is growing as I realize how perfectly you understand and how carefully you watch over my life. Thank you for staying with me.

January 14

O perfect love, all human thought transcending,
lowly we kneel in prayer before thy throne.
That theirs may be the love
which knows no ending,
whom Thou for evermore dost join in one.
O perfect life, be thou their full assurance of
tender charity and steadfast faith,
of patient hope, and quiet, brave endurance,
with childlike trust that fears
nor pain nor death.
Grant them the joy
which brightens earthly sorrow,
grant them the peace
which calms all earthly strife, and to life's day
the glorious unknown morrow
that dawns upon eternal love and life.

—Dorothy Gurney, "O Perfect Love"

January 15

Lord, when I am navigating deep waters, your Word is my beacon. You keep me from going far astray. Let me always see your light and your grace acting in my life.

January 16

O Holy Creator, who hath bound together heaven and earth, let me walk through your kingdom comforted and protected by the warm rays of your love. Let me be healed as I stand basking in the divine light of your presence, where strength and hope and joy are found. Let me sit at rest in the valley of your peace, surrounded by the fortress of your loving care.

January 17

Let, I pray thee, thy merciful kindness be for my comfort, according to thy word unto thy servant. Let thy tender mercies come unto me.

—Psalm 119:76–77

January 18

Faith is the root of all blessings. Believe and you shall be saved; believe and you will be satisfied; believe, and you cannot but be comforted and happy.

—Jeremy Taylor

January 19

Thank you for the morning light.

Thank you for this day today.

Thank you for my daily bread.

Thank you for the sights I see.

Thank you for the air I breathe.

Thank you as the evening comes.

Thank you as sleep falls.

—Anonymous

January 20

Lord God, I experience your comforting love for me in so many ways. Cards and phone calls come from friends and family who want to tell me they are thinking of me and praying for me. You send a timely message to me in the form of a poem, an article, a sermon. And just seeing or being in your creation holds a special healing balm for my soul. Thank you, Father. All these things tell me again and again: You are near.

Now the God of hope fill you with all joy and peace in believing, that ye may abound in hope, through the power of the Holy Ghost.

—Romans 15:13

God, you know I need a little hope today! Some days it is easy for me to believe in your love. Other days, I need a little boost. Please help me today!

January 22

Now faith is the substance of things hoped for, the evidence of things not seen.

—Hebrews 11:1

Father, I admit that I have given up hope sometimes because I have misplaced my hopes and have made demands on you and others that I have no right to make. Please heal my disappointment and fear. Teach me how to place my hope in you the way the Bible reveals I can. I'm looking forward to learning how to walk this new path with you.

January 23

If you do not hope, you will not find what is beyond your hopes.

—St. Clement of Alexandria

Lord, give me hope,
Give me patience to cope
And a reason to keep on trying.
Take my trembling hand
Give me power to stand
And a faith that is strong and undying.

But that on the good ground are they, which in an honest and good heart, having heard the word, keep it, and bring forth fruit with patience.

—Luke 8:15

When you come to the end of your rope, and patience seems to fly away, settle back into God's waiting arms.

January 25

Then shalt thou walk in thy way safely, and thy foot shall not stumble.

—Proverbs 3:23

If you find stumbling blocks in your path, use them as stepping stones to move closer to the good in life.

Nothing shall be impossible unto you.

—Matthew 17:20

Just a tiny seed of faith, watered with love, wisdom, and hard work, grows into a majestic tree of blessings.

January 27

My Father, grant me renewed hope in you alone. Forgive me for misplacing my hope in things that are not you. I know you are faithful, that you never fail, and that you are worthy of my devotion. When my hope ebbs away, let your goodness flow into my life to help me remain steadfast. Thank you that you are here walking with me in my circumstances. I look past everything that is threatening to trouble me right now and will abide in true hope. You are my hope. Amen

January 28

Count neither the hours nor the seconds
That filled your mind with doubts and fears.
Do not add up unhappy moments,
when pain and hardships brought you to tears.
Regard not days on faded calendars
that marked the passage of your years.
Instead, count heaven's blessings...
grandchildren playing on the floor,
old friends walking through the door,
white clouds drifting up above,
and, like a faithful timepiece, God's love.

January 29

Beautiful pastel colors,
pink, blue, golden, white,
Brightening every highway and byway,
colors soft and light.
Covering the earth in a rosy glow,
a special sunset for all to see.
Brushstrokes of heavenly beauty
on a canvas that spans the seas.
I can't describe my feelings
as I watch him paint the sky,
A sense of solace covers the earth
as another day goes by.

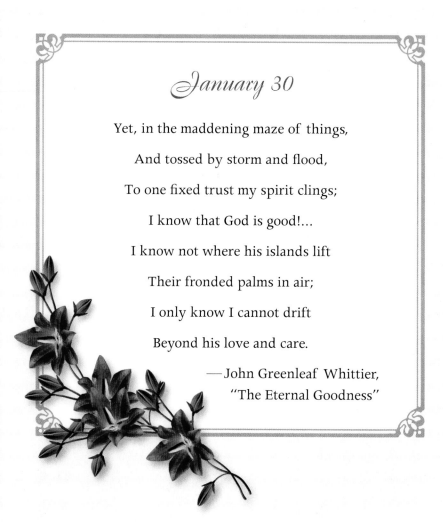

January 30

Yet, in the maddening maze of things,

And tossed by storm and flood,

To one fixed trust my spirit clings;

I know that God is good!...

I know not where his islands lift

Their fronded palms in air;

I only know I cannot drift

Beyond his love and care.

—John Greenleaf Whittier,
"The Eternal Goodness"

January 31

God of my life, the
darkness of my grief
cannot shut out the
light of your com-
forting love. It glows
softly, warmly even
as I weep, and I know
that you are holding
me close. Thank you
for staying with me
through this dark
night. I know that you
will carry me to a place
of consolation and
then, one day, to joy
again. But for now, I'm
satisfied just to know
the soothing tender-
ness of your presence
that causes me to
know I am not walking
this path alone.

February

February 1

The secret to happiness lies within the present moment. Only in the immediate here and now will we find our life waiting to happen. It is impossible to live last week or experience next month. Yesterday is dead, and tomorrow is but a hoped-for event. Wise is the soul that cherishes this day, this hour, this moment, and does not long for other times. Fortunate is the heart that loves what is right in front of it, not what it once had or wishes it could have. And blessed is the mind that worries not over what was or what might someday be, but focuses entirely on what is.

February 2

I've traveled down the road of life,
Enjoyed its pleasures and weathered its strife.
I dearly pray that I have not squandered
All those miles so hastily wandered.
For I cannot erase one ill-used time
Nor change its waste to righteous prime.
I must journey on, around each new bend,
Until I have reached my destiny's end,
Where only you, dear Lord, can tell
If I have done my traveling well.

February 3

Faith, mighty faith, the promise sees,
And looks to that alone;
Laughs at impossibilities,
And cries it shall be done.

—Charles Wesley

February 4

When hope seems gone, I spy doves like those God sent Noah to assure him the storm was subsiding. Doves of inspiration, knowledge, understanding; doves in the shape of those not letting me travel alone. I'm energized for the rest of the journey. Land is in sight.

February 5

For thou shalt eat the labour of thine hands:
happy shalt thou be, and it shall be well
with thee.

—Psalm 128:2

There is in the worst of fortune the best chances for a
happy change.

—Euripides

February 6

If I have my friends, I have all the wealth I desire.

If I have my health, I have all the power I need.

If I have my family, I have all the love I want.

If I have my purpose, I have all the meaning I crave.

If I have my self-respect,

I have all the confidence I require.

If I have God's wisdom, I have all the answers I seek.

February 7

O love the Lord, all ye his saints: for the Lord preserveth the faithful, and plentifully re-wardeth the proud doer.

—Psalm 31:23

Nothing great was ever accomplished by sitting in the stands. In order to experience life fully, I must get into the race and risk being bumped, sidelined, and put out of commission for a while. But at least I will have tried. At least I will have dared. At least I will have dreamed.

February 8

Kindness is perhaps the most underrated and underused of all the virtues. People often don't have the time or energy for gestures of goodness and compassion. Yet the simple act of doing something for someone else is like a contagious epidemic that, when it spreads, threatens to bring about world peace.

February 9

Sometimes the path ahead seems rocky and
steep. God, I call to you to set my steps firmly
so I do not take a tumble. I ask you to guide me
past obstacles. And I hope that I will look up to
see beauty all around me!

February 10

Lord, help me to depend on you to be my source of goodness. I don't always feel like being patient, kind, loving, or joyful, but you are all of these things by your very nature. So right now I place my strengths and weaknesses into your hands, asking you to infuse them with yourself and to make them instruments of good that will serve others for your sake.

It is never too late

to tell someone you love them.

It is never too late

to try the thing, you've always wanted to do.

It is never too late

to begin all over again.

It is never too late

to fall in love with your life.

It is never too late

to take better care of yourself.

It is never too late

to give to those who have less.

It is never too late

to share your gifts with the world.

It is never too late

to go after your dreams.

So, start, now, today, this minute.

Before it's too late.

February 12

The Lord render to every man his righteousness and his faithfulness; for the Lord delivered thee into my hand to day, but I would not stretch forth mine hand against the Lord's anointed.

—1 Samuel 26:23

Every moment we are alive is full of reasons to sing out in joyful gratitude. Every breath we are given is a reminder that the glory of life is at hand. In the people we love, in the beauty of nature, in the golden sun that rises each morning—miracles are everywhere.

February 13

Dear God, what would you like me to do today? I have my own ideas, but I would most of all like to do your will. Is there anyone you would like me to reach out to, so that they know that they are not alone? Is there a conversation I need to have with a family member? I am going to sit in silence with you for a while, waiting for you to inspire my heart.

February 14

Happy is that people, that is in such a case: yea, happy is that people, whose God is the Lord.

—Psalm 144:15

Silent prayer with you is a delight, but so is shared worship with my church community. When I am feeling alone, let me remember that others are on this journey too.

February 15

When it comes to life, there's good news and there's bad news. The good news is you can change your life. The bad news is you must learn how to use that power correctly, in accordance with God's will. The good news is you've been given free will. The bad news is you must be disciplined enough to use it. The good news is that you are loved. The bad news is that you can turn away from that love. The good news is that you can always turn back, running like the Prodigal Son back into your Father's arms. The good news is that your Father will be with you, every step of the way along your journey, as long as you reach out and ask for his help and grace.

February 16

If life is a classroom,
these are the lessons:
Pay attention.
Listen closely to your teachers.
Ask for help.
Share what you learned with others.
Never stop learning or sharing.
Take time out for rest.
Play well with others.
Think before you speak or act.
Always tell the truth.
Don't cheat.
Do your own work.
Do it well.
Be kind to others—and to yourself.
Be yourself.
Use your head.
Follow your heart.

February 17

For the Lord God is a sun and shield: the Lord will give grace and glory: no good thing will he withhold from them that walk uprightly.

—Psalm 84:11

Peace comes to those who know it is an inward state of mind, not an outward state of being. When we've attained inner balance and harmony with God, nothing that occurs outside of us can disrupt that claim. Those who have the true peace of Christ know that they can meet both good fortune and misfortune with a positive attitude and achieve an equally positive outcome. Inner peace depends not on outer circumstance, but on our reactions.

February 18

Now the God of patience and consolation grant you to be likeminded one toward another according to Christ Jesus

—Romans 15:5

February 19

To let go is to live.
Letting go of old
sins and habits
opens the way for
you to begin re-
ceiving more grace.
Imagine a tree that
refused to shed its
dead leaves. Where
would the new
leaves find room to
bloom? Without
an outlet for new
growth, eventually
the whole tree suf-
fers. By getting rid
of the old to make
way for the new, the
whole tree benefits.

February 20

She is a tree of life to them that lay hold upon her: and happy is every one that retaineth her.

—Proverbs 3:18

Lord, please grant me your wisdom today, for I am feeling at sea and a little foolish. Did I trust the wrong person? Where am I not seeing clearly? Please guide me.

February 21

Tonight, there was a shooting star—a bright arc of star-light sprinting into the darkness. I looked for a trace of it, to no avail. There was no trail against the deep dusk. No scar in the atmosphere. And as I mused at what I had seen, the "fixed fires"—the other stars—burned on.

Some people, though sweeping swiftly like a shooting star through our lives, can be a wonderful presence that stirs our imagination and awakens our sleeping sense of adventure. Other people are more like the stars that appear each night: always with us, faithful to the end. Which of these do we need the most in our experience? Perhaps the answer is both. For each has its own kind of light that infuses our life with joy and blessing. Thank you, God, for both.

February 22

The fearful mind sees limitations and accepts them as obstacles that cannot be overcome. The mind inspired by God sees those same limitations and accepts them as challenges—challenges that can become opportunities to move out beyond the comfort zone and into a realm of pure potential and limitless possibilities.

Then Jacob went on his journey, and came into
the land of the people of the east.

—Genesis 29:1

Mark Twain wrote that an optimist is someone who
"travels on nothing from nowhere to happiness." When I
seem to have nothing, Lord, I know I have you!

February 24

I will speak of the glorious honour of thy majesty, and of thy wondrous works.

—Psalm 145:5

Good things come to those who wait, but great things come to those who pursue their dreams in accordance with God's will. With clarity of heart and God's help, anything can be achieved. Take that first step forward, and watch your deepest dreams come rushing to meet you like an old friend.

February 25

There is a fine line between helping each other person and making them dependent on us. We can help a bird with a broken wing by wrapping the injury, but we cannot make that bird fly. That is up to the bird. We can support a friend who wants to go after dream, but we cannot go after that dream for them. That is up to our friend. To truly help another person, we need to guide them to help themselves and place their trust in God. Then, and only then, will they be able to become healed, whole, and empowered.

February 26

We will go three days' journey into the wilderness, and sacrifice to the Lord our God, as he shall command us.

—Exodus 8:27

Spreading your great branches
Over all who come,
Sheltering humble hearts
From judgment's burning sun.
Here your shade of mercy
Stirs breezes deep within.
In heaven's center planted
We find you once again.

February 27

God, I couldn't help noticing all the loveliness you placed in the world today! This morning I witnessed a sunrise that made my heart beat faster. Then, later, I watched a father gently help his child across a busy parking lot; his tenderness was much like yours. While inside a department store, I spied an elderly couple sitting on a bench. I could hear the man cracking jokes; their laughter lifted my spirits. Then early this evening, I walked by a woman tending her flower bed; she took great pleasure in her work, and her garden was breathtaking. Later, I talked with a friend who is helping some needy families; her genuine compassion inspired me. Thank you, Lord, for everything that is beautiful and good in the world.

February 28

And Enoch walked with God: and he was not;
for God took him.

—Genesis 5:24

After making plans to go hiking with friends, I remembered my boots were a half size too small. My budget, however, was telling me that new footwear was out of the question. Without much hope, I decided to visit a sporting-goods store. As I drove there, I spotted a thrift store and felt a strong impulse to stop in. "God, please let there be a good pair of hiking boots in my size here," I prayed. Scanning the rows of shoes, I found only one pair of authentic hiking boots, and they were in new condition. But would they fit? I fumbled to find the sizing information. When I read it, I wanted to let out a whoop, but instead I whispered, "Thank you, God!" Then, handing the cashier a mere eight dollars and some change, I couldn't help but say "Thank you" again.

February 29

Being in the flow of life means letting things happen in God's timing, not yours. When you try to force things to happen, you're met with resistance, and you run up against numerous obstacles. You end up taking detours that waste your time and energy, and your enthusiasm wanes as the task becomes more difficult. Often you end up making something happen, only to find that it wasn't what you really wanted to have happen! But if you just relax and go with the flow of life, the natural order of things takes over, and divine timing kicks into gear. Life becomes harmonious, and enjoyable, just as it was meant to be.

March

March 1

Then he said unto them, Go your way, eat the fat, and drink the sweet, and send portions unto them for whom nothing is prepared: for this day is holy unto our Lord: neither be ye sorry; for the joy of the Lord is your strength.

—Nehemiah 8:10

When you feel unsure about the future, remember that God has given you the strength to make it this far, and that therefore, you have what it takes to travel all the way.

March 2

The Lord is my strength and song, and he is become my salvation: he is my God, and I will prepare him an habitation; my father's God, and I will exalt him.

—Exodus 15:2

When we draw a circle around ourselves to shut him out, God draws a larger circle to take us in.

March 3

I spend a lot of time—too much time—thinking, "If only."
If only I had that possession, I would be happier. If only
someone would stop doing something that annoys me, I
would be happier. If only the world would arrange itself
exactly to my liking, I would be happier! Lord, teach me
contentment in the present moment, and in your presence.
For true contentment is found when thy will, not mine,
is done.

March 4

March is the window to nature's most joyous season.

March 5

We're starting to see the first tentative signs of spring.
It's been a long winter, Lord, both weather-wise and
sometimes spiritually. My eyes and my heart are ready for
renewal and new life. Please prepare my heart to receive
you in a new way as we head towards the Easter season of
new beginnings and new life.

March 6

God, your love for me is a gift. I thank you for that gift. I give you my heart too!

March 7

Let my refrain today be simple: Praise you, God! In good times and bad, praise you, God!

March 8

But they that wait upon the Lord shall renew their strength; they shall mount up with wings as eagles; they shall run, and not be weary; and they shall walk, and not faint.

—Isaiah 40:31

Lord, I am surely in need of renewal. It's a lesson I learn again and again: When I rely on my own strength, I inevitably grow weary. When I act on my own timing, and not yours, I grow faint. Today, I wait on your guidance.

March 9

Stand in a beloved's shade, not shadow, and discover new sights to share, new directions to go, all leading to even more reasons for standing together.

March 10

Whenever you take a journey, whether across town to a familiar home or across the country to a new place, remember to take an angel with you. The angel will guide your path, watch your steps, and keep you company all along the way.

March 11

The righteous cry, and the Lord heareth, and
delivereth them out of all their troubles.

—Psalm 34:17

Lord, I am troubled today. Will you reach out to me in a
way I can recognize? I need your help.

March 12

I trust God's plan;
I know he made me—

What a wonder I turned out to be!

I'm not too short...
And I'm not too tall...
Just the way he planned it all.

He planned I'd be kind,
he planned I'd be good—
but I'd be even better if I could.

Sometimes I goof up;
sometimes I get mad;
But I know I wasn't made to be bad.

I keep trying harder
to be loving and kind—
I know that's the plan God had in mind.

I like to make smiles,
I like to get hugs,
I like giving someone's heart a good tug.

It makes me feel happy
helping out when I can—
I know for sure that was part of his plan.

In this whole wide world
there is no other me,
so, I try to be the best me I can be!

March 13

In the day when I cried thou answeredst me,
and strengthenedst me with strength in my soul.

—Psalm 138:3

We must wait for God...Wait, and he will come.

—Frederick Faber

March 14

We can live without many things, but we cannot live without hope. Yet, when life's circumstances deal us one discouraging blow after another, hope can get knocked right out of us. Sometimes it can feel as if we don't even have a breath left to lift a prayer. "Why bother," we tell ourselves. "It's hopeless." That is an old fatal lie that we must resist with our last ounce of strength. As long as there is a breath of life in us, there is hope. Why? Because there is a God, and he is good.

March 15

I have set the Lord always before me: because
he is at my right hand, I shall not be moved.

—Psalm 16:8

With his daily work and his books, many a man whom the
world thought forlorn has found life worth living.

—Charles W. Eliot

March 16

Walk in the light! So, you shall know
that fellowship of love.
His Spirit only can bestow,
who reigns in light above...
Walk in the light! And you shall find
your heart made truly his,
who dwells in cloudless light enshrined,
in whom no darkness is.
Walk in the light! And yours shall be
a path, though thorny, bright.
For God, by grace, shall dwell in thee,
and God himself is light.

—Bernard Barton, Adapted

March 17

It matters not how long you live, but how well.

—Publius Syrus

March 18

When my life-work is ended,
and I cross the swelling tide,
when the bright and glorious
morning I shall see,
I shall know my Redeemer when
I reach the other side,
and his smile will be the first to
welcome me.
Oh, the soul thrilling rapture when I
view his blessed face,
and the luster of his kindly beaming eye!
How my full soul shall praise him for the
mercy, love, and grace
that prepare for me a mansion in the sky.
Through the gates to the city in a robe
of spotless white,
he will lead me where no tears
shall ever fall.
In the glad songs of ages,
I shall mingle with delight;
but I long to meet my Savior first of all.

—Fanny Crosby

March 19

God, your creations bring me delight! When I slow down, a walk through the neighborhood becomes a joy to my senses, filled with beautiful sights and sounds. You are the great artist, spreading color and light everywhere!

March 20

Truly my soul waiteth upon God: from him cometh my salvation. He only is my rock and my salvation; he is my defence; I shall not be greatly moved.

—Psalm 62:1–2

Walk boldly into the future. Through all its uncertain paths and unknown destinations, God will guide you. The thrill of new adventure and challenges await you.

March 21

Lord, may I be wakeful at sunrise to begin a new day for you, cheerful at sunset for having done my work for you; thankful at moonrise and under starshine for the beauty of the universe. And may I add what little may be in me to your great world.

—The Abbot of Greve

March 22

When you are in the dark, listen, and God will give you a very precious message for someone else when you get into the light.

—Oswald Chambers

March 23

Lord, you are here,

Lord, you are there.

You are wherever we go.

Lord, you guide us,

Lord, you protect us.

You are wherever we go.

Lord, we need you,

Lord, we trust you,

You are wherever we go.

Lord, we love you,

Lord, we praise you,

You are wherever we go.

March 24

For thou wilt light my candle: the Lord my God will enlighten my darkness. For by thee I have run through a troop; and by my God have I leaped over a wall.

—Psalm 18:28–29

Recently, I was hiking through a canyon with a friend. A couple was approaching us on the trail from the opposite direction. They were holding hands, and their heads were bowed together as if they were sharing a secret.

The woman seemed shy and chuckling from under locks of shiny black hair. The man, with silvery-black hair, was quite handsome. They had a youthful, energetic glow despite being up in years.

As we got closer to them on the trail, we could see the man's eyes shining with love. As we passed him, he said with a huge grin, "I'm in heaven when she giggles."

My friend and I smiled and responded, "He's a keeper!"

By this time the couple had passed us. The man called out, "Thirty-three years! And I'm still in heaven!"

We both felt touched to have witnessed such a love and to be reminded that is possible. Heaven on earth really does exist.

March 26

One person who has mastered life is better than a thousand persons who have mastered only the contents of books, but no one can get anything out of life without God.

— Meister Eckhardt

March 27

O most merciful Lord, grant to me thy grace,
that it may be with me, and labour with me, and
persevere with me even to the end. Grant that I
may always desire and will that which is to thee
most acceptable, and most dear. Let thy will be
mine, and my will ever follow thine, and agree
perfectly with it. Grant to me above all things
that can be desired, to rest in thee, and in thee
to have my heart at peace.

—Thomas à Kempis

March 28

Over mountains and over valleys and over oceans and over rivers and over deserts one says: Blessed are you, Lord, our God, king of the world, who makes the works of creation... Over rain and over good news one says: Blessed are You, Lord, our God, ruler of the world, who is God and who does good things.

And for bad news one says: Blessed are You, Lord, our God, ruler of the world, who is the true judge.

—The Talmud, Blessings, Berakhot 9:2

March 29

Be strong and of a good courage, fear not, nor
be afraid of them: for the Lord thy God, he it is
that doth go with thee; he will not fail thee, nor
forsake thee.

—Deuteronomy 31:6

When you have no helpers, see all your helpers in God.
When you have many helpers, see God in all your helpers.
When you have nothing but God, see all in God; when you
have everything, see God in everything. Under all condi-
tions, stay thy heart only on the Lord.

—Charles Haddon Spurgeon

March 30

He giveth power to the faint; and to them that
have no might he increaseth strength.

—Isaiah 40:29

You have made us for yourself and our hearts are restless
until they rest in you.

—St. Augustine of Hippo

March 31

One there is, above all others,
well deserves the name of friend;
his is love beyond a brother's,
costly, free, and knows no end;
they who once his kindness proves
find it everlasting love.
O for grace our hearts to soften!
Teach us, Lord, at length to love;
we, alas! forget too often
what a Friend we have above;
but when home our souls are brought,
we will love You as we ought.

—John Newton,
"One There Is, Above All Others"

April

April 1

It is a time of hope! Lord, I wait for you in hope. I ask for my prayer intentions in hope, trusting that you will answer them however it is best. I see signs of hope around me, in the budding trees and the returning flowers. I feel hope within me, as I contemplate what in my life has grown stale, what needs to change.

April 2

Every man according as he purposeth in his heart, so let him give.

—2 Corinthians 9:7

Give what you have. To some it may be better than you dare think.

—Henry Wadsworth Longfellow

April 3

Lord, how would you like me to love my neighbor today?
Is there someone in my life that I don't think of as a neighbor whom you are calling me to love? Please let me be open
to widening my definition, as the Good Samaritan reached
out to a hurt man who would traditionally have been his
nemesis. Sometimes, walking with you means walking with
people I would not expect!

April 4

In everything give thanks: for this is the will of
God in Christ Jesus concerning you.

— 1 Thessalonians 5:18

If the only prayer you say in your entire life is "thank
you," that would suffice.

— Meister Eckhart

One of the great men of faith in the Bible is Job, who lost his children and his wealth. Moreover, his health took such a turn for the worse that his wife encouraged him to just give up and die. Yet, Job remained faithful to the Lord. His secret had everything to do with his relationship with God. Job was confident—confident even while he grieved—that however great and painful his losses in this life, he would never become lost in despair as long as his God was walking with him.

April 6

God of love,
bless this family.
Guard our house,
Guard our bodies,
Guard our souls.
Let us be peaceful,
Let us be be healthy,
Let us be loving.
In the name of Jesus Christ,
we pray.
Amen

—Anonymous

April 7

To be with God, there is no need to be continually in church. We may make [a chapel] of our heart. . .to converse with him in meekness, humility, and love. There is not in the world a kind of life more sweet and delightful than that of a continual conversation with God.

—Brother Lawrence

April 8

Lord Jesus, you are medicine to me when I
am sick, strength to me when I need help, life
itself when I fear death, the way when I long
for heaven, the light when all is dark, and food
when I need nourishment. Glory be to you forever. Amen.

—Saint Ambrose

April 9

Lord God, I'm grateful today for all that you have given me, and I rejoice in the blessing of life. Help me see how you intend to enrich my life by my losses; help me see them from an eternal perspective. I want to learn to relate to you and others on a deeper, more meaningful level because of my trials. Help me in this, I pray. Amen.

April 10

And Thomas answered and said unto him, My Lord and my God.

—John 20:28

April 11

And it shall be forgiven all the congregation of the children of Israel, and the stranger that sojourneth among them; seeing all the people were in ignorance.

—Numbers 15:26

April 12

Have all the gifts of healing? do all speak with tongues? do all interpret?

—1 Corinthians 12:30

Lord, thank you for the spiritual gifts you have given me. Please let me know what they are, share them with others, and not be jealous of the gifts of others.

April 13

In the midst of the street of it, and on either
side of the river, was there the tree of life,
which bare twelve manner of fruits, and yield-
ed her fruit every month: and the leaves of the
tree were for the healing of the nations.

—Revelation 22:2

April 14

Dear God, in my struggle with losing things I hold dear, please help me. I long for your comfort and for a renewed sense of joy and gratitude for the good gifts you have given me. Help me focus on the things of eternal value and to praise you for each one. I'll start by thanking you for my salvation. All else may become lost, but my life belongs to you forever because you have found me and will always walk with me. I praise you for this!

April 15

The mighty God, even the Lord, hath spoken, and called the earth from the rising of the sun unto the going down thereof.

—Psalm 50:1

I am weak, but thou art mighty; hold me with thy powerful hand.

—William Williams

April 16

I believe, God, that you give us faith as a means of getting in touch with your love. For once we have that love, we can pass it on to others.

—Henry Drummond

April 17

Be ye therefore followers of God, as dear children; And walk in love, as Christ also hath loved us, and hath given himself for us an offering and a sacrifice to God for a sweetsmelling savour.

—Ephesians 5:1–2

April 18

Father, I take hold of you today. Grant me faith and confidence in your good plans for my life. Help me wait expectantly for you to show me the path of life today. I will count my blessings, find reasons to praise you, and walk in gratitude with you. Amen.

April 19

And thou shalt be secure, because there is hope;
yea, thou shalt dig about thee, and thou shalt
take thy rest in safety.

—Job 11:18

There are no hopeless situations; there are only men who
have grown hopeless about them.

—Clara Boothe Luce

April 20

Merciful God, you have poured out many good gifts on my life, and I thank you for each one. Thank you, too, for the gifts that you have given me only for a season. I acknowledge your right to give and to take away, and I even rejoice in it, because I know that you are always seeking to bless me. Help me trust your goodness and your love for me as you walk with me, now and always. Amen.

April 21

If your body suffers pain, and your health you
can't regain, and your soul is almost sinking in
despair, Jesus knows the pain you feel, he can
save and he can heal, take your burden to the
Lord and leave it there.

—Charles Albert Tindley

April 22

Let thy mercy, O Lord, be upon us, according as we hope in thee.

—Psalm 33:22

Hope is the best possession. None are completely wretched but those who are without hope.

—William Hazlitt

April 23

Save me, O God; for the waters are come in unto my soul. I sink in deep mire, where there is no standing: I am come into deep waters, where the floods overflow me. I am weary of my crying: my throat is dried: mine eyes fail while I wait for my God.

—Psalm 69:1–3

April 24

Life is short and we have never too much time
for gladdening the hearts of those who are trav-
elling the dark journey with us. Oh, be swift to
love, make haste to be kind.

—Henri Frederic Amiel

April 25

The prophet that hath a dream, let him tell a
dream; and he that hath my word, let him speak
my word faithfully. What is the chaff to the
wheat? saith the Lord.

—Jeremiah 23:28

Faith is the ear of the soul.

—Clement of Alexandria

April 26

I falter where I firmly trod,
And falling with my weight of cares
Upon the great world's altar stairs
That slope through darkness up to God,
I stretch lame hands of faith, and grope,
And gather dust and chaff, and call
To what I feel is Lord of all,
And faintly trust the larger hope.

—Alfred, Lord Tennyson

April 27

And he charged them, saying, Thus shall ye do in the fear of the Lord, faithfully, and with a perfect heart.

—2 Chronicles 19:9

A life of faith...enables us to see God in everything and it holds the mind in a state of readiness for whatever may be his will.

—François Fénelon

April 28

Count your blessings, name them one by one:
Count your blessings, see what God hath done.
Count your blessings, name them one by one;
Count your many blessings, see what God
hath done.

—Johnson Oatman, Jr.,
"Count Your Blessings"

April 29

The Lord appeared to Abram, and said unto him, I am the Almighty God; walk before me, and be thou perfect.

—Genesis 17:1

April 30

Let me but live my life from year to year,

With forward face and unreluctantly soul;

Not hurrying to, nor turning from, the goal;

Not mourning for the things that disappear

In the dim past, nor holding back in fear

From what the future veils; but with a whole

And happy heart, that pays its toll

To Youth and Age, and travels on with cheer.

—Henry Van Dyke

May

In thankfulness for present mercy, nothing so becomes us as losing sight of past ills.

—Lew Wallace

May 2

It is like a grain of mustard seed, which, when it is sown in the earth, is less than all the seeds that be in the earth.

—Mark 4:31

A Chinese proverb says, "All the flowers of all the tomorrows are in the seeds of today." Lord, please let my faith flower!

May 3

And out of the ground made the Lord God to grow every tree that is pleasant to the sight, and good for food; the tree of life also in the midst of the garden, and the tree of knowledge of good and evil.

—Genesis 2:9

Do not rule out God's help with the small details of life. After all, details make up the totality of life. If we do not let God into our everyday lives, he may not be able to intervene in the crises.

—Catherine Marshall

May 4

I have been apart and I have lost my way... And in my hours of darkness when I am not even sure there is a Thou hearing my call, I still call to Thee with all my heart. Hear the cry of my voice, clamoring from this desert, for my soul is parched and my heart can barely stand this longing.

—Traditional

May 5

And the Lord God formed man of the dust of the ground, and breathed into his nostrils the breath of life; and man became a living soul.

—Genesis 2:7

There is no great and no small
To the soul that maketh all;
And where it cometh, all things are;
And it cometh everywhere.

—Ralph Waldo Emerson

May 6

Is anything too hard for the Lord? At the time appointed I will return unto thee, according to the time of life, and Sarah shall have a son.

—Genesis 18:14

God gives the shoulder according to the burden.

—German proverb

May 7

Bless to me, O God, the earth beneath my feet,
Bless to me, O God, the path whereon I go,
Bless to me, O God, the people whom I meet,
Today, tonight and tomorrow.

—Celtic Blessing

And there stood no man with him, while Joseph made himself known unto his brethren. And he wept aloud.

—Genesis 45:1–2

Sometimes people, even our own family members, hurt us deeply. Lord, when I feel I have been hurt beyond the possibility of reconciliation, please lead the one who hurt me to true repentence and show me a path to forgiveness. You are a restoring God, who wants to make us whole.

May 9

And Moses called all Israel, and said unto them, Hear, O Israel, the statutes and judgments which I speak in your ears this day, that ye may learn them, and keep, and do them.

—Deuteronomy 5:1

Your holy scriptures speak to us today, through the generations. I want always to desire to follow your will.

May 10

Sometimes the simplest prayers are all that is needed. Today I cry out, "Lord, I believe, help my unbelief!"

May 11

O Lord, seek us, O Lord, find us
in thy patient care;
be thy love before, behind us,
round us, everywhere:
Lest the god of this world blind us,
lest he speak us fair,
lest he forge a chain to bind us,
lest he bait a snare.
Turn not from us, call to mind us,
find, embrace us, bear;
be thy love before, behind us,
round us everywhere.

—Christina Rossetti

May 12

And thou shalt eat before the Lord thy God, in the place which he shall choose to place his name there, the tithe of thy corn, of thy wine, and of thine oil, and the firstlings of thy herds and of thy flocks; that thou mayest learn to fear the Lord thy God always.

—Deuteronomy 14:23

May 13

Give instruction to a wise man, and he will be yet wiser: teach a just man, and he will increase in learning.

—Proverbs 9:9

I have a decision before me. I ask for your guidance, that it be a wise decision that leads me to act justly.

May 14

The road to a friend's house is never long.

—Danish proverb

May 15

Learn to do well; seek judgment, relieve the oppressed, judge the fatherless, plead for the widow.

—Isaiah 1:17

So many people are grieving, Lord. They feel alone. After a death, support drops away after the first few weeks or months. Is there anyone I should reach out to today?

May 16

A man that hath friends must shew himself friendly: and there is a friend that sticketh closer than a brother.

—Proverbs 18:24

How lucky I am to have known someone who was so hard to say goodbye to.

—Unknown

May 17

All the service that weighs an ounce in the sight of God is that which is prompted by love.

—Billy Sunday

May 18

They also that erred in spirit shall come to understanding, and they that murmured shall learn doctrine.

—Isaiah 29:24

Lord, where I have walked away from you, please correct my ways. I know you always invite me to return to you.

May 19

Thank you for gardeners, God! Thank you who toil to make a beautiful landscape that we can all enjoy, who love your beautiful creation!

May 20

Continue patiently, believingly, perseveringly to wait upon God.

—George Muller

May 21

He is a loving, tender hand, full of sympathy
and compassion.

—Dwight L. Moody

May 22

But the stranger that dwelleth with you shall
be unto you as one born among you, and thou
shalt love him as thyself; for ye were strangers
in the land of Egypt: I am the Lord your God.

—Leviticus 19:34

Please give us all a generous heart for the refugees among
us, fleeing oppressive governments or natural disasters.
Please give those who have been uprooted a new home.

May 23

The heart of the wise teacheth his mouth, and addeth learning to his lips.

—Proverbs 16:23

When I think I know it all, when I think I can lecture others about how to behave—Lord, grant me humility!

And because he loved thy fathers, therefore he chose their seed after them, and brought thee out in his sight with his mighty power out of Egypt.

—Deuteronomy 4:37

What trust it must have taken, to walk towards the Red Sea with Moses. God, please grant me that kind of trust.

May 25

O may thy spirit guide my feet in ways of righteousness; make every path of duty straight, and plain before my face.
Amen.

—Joachim Neander

May 26

Though long the weary way we tread, and sorrow crown each lingering year, no path we shun, no darkness dread, our hearts still whispering, thou art near!

—Oliver Wendell Holmes

May 27

All the great blessings of my life
Are present in my thoughts today.

—Phoebe Cary

May 28

In this month of May, thank you for mothers, grand-mothers, and aunts--all those women of faith who have walked before me!

May 29

He that cannot forgive others, breaks the bridge over which he himself must pass if he would ever reach heaven, for everyone has need to be forgiven.

—George Herbert

God, please free me of this grudge that I am holding. I can't quite let go of it on my own. I need the help of your Holy Spirit to forgive as you forgave!

May 30

For pathways, walkways, sidewalks, and hiking trails, I
thank you today, O Creator God!

May 31

And he will love thee, and bless thee, and multiply thee: he will also bless the fruit of thy womb, and the fruit of thy land, thy corn, and thy wine, and thine oil, the increase of thy kine, and the flocks of thy sheep, in the land which he sware unto thy fathers to give thee.

—Deuteronomy 7:13

I don't always believe in or trust your promises. Let me take a step forward in faith today. You want good for me!

June

June 1

Were there no God, we would be in this glorious world with grateful hearts: and no one to thank.

—Christina Rossetti

June 2

Faith laughs at the shaking of the spear; unbelief trembles at the shaking of a leaf, unbelief starves the soul; faith finds food in famine, and a table in the wilderness.

—Robert Cecil

Whatever I fear I lift up to your hands, O Lord. Whatever I worry about, I lift up to your hands, O Lord. Whatever I regret, I lift up to your hands, O Lord.

June 3

Everything has its wonders, even darkness and silence, and I learn, whatever state I may be in, therein to be content.

—Helen Keller,
"The Story of My Life"

June 4

Teach us, good Lord, to serve Thee as Thou deservest. To give and not to count the cost.

—St. Ignatius Loyola

June 5

When my way is drear, Precious Lord, linger near.

When the day is almost gone,

hear my cry, hear my call,

hold my hand, lest I fall,

precious Lord, take my hand, lead me home.

June 6

These things I have spoken unto you, that in me ye might have peace. In the world ye shall have tribulation: but be of good cheer; I have overcome the world.

—John 16:33

Getting out into nature often makes my problems seem so small. Your creation is so grand, and your love so great!

June 7

Deliver me, O God, from a slothful mind, from all lukewarmness, and all dejection of spirit. I know these cannot but deaden my love to you.

—John Wesley

June 8

Over my head—I hear music in the air...
Over my head—I hear singing in the air...
There must be a God somewhere.

—Traditional spiritual

June 9

And the man wondering at her held his peace,
to wit whether the Lord had made his journey
prosperous or not.

— Genesis 24:21

Abraham sent a servant out on a journey to seek Rebekah.
Lord, let me entrust my family to your guiding hand.

June 10

Peace in the soul is the consciousness that, however difficult life may be, we are not living it alone.

—Harry Emerson Fosdick

June 11

Clay on the wheel, let the fingers of the divine potter model you at their will. Obey the Father's lightest word: hear the Brother who knows you and died for you.

—George MacDonald

June 12

Multitudes, multitudes in the valley of decision: for the day of the Lord is near in the valley of decision.

—Joel 3:14

When things seem dark, let me remember your gracious promises. In the Bible, people dealt with despair, war, and exile—yet you were still there for them.

June 13

I have resolved to pray more and pray always,
to pray in all places where quietness inviteth:
in the house, on the highway and on the street.

—Sir Thomas Browne

June 14

If I have wounded any soul today,
If I have caused one foot to go astray,
If I have walked in my own willful way,
Dear Lord, forgive!

—C. Maude Battersby

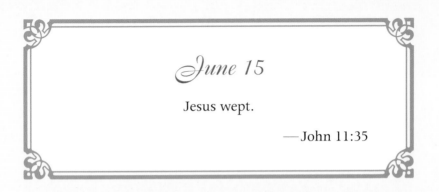

June 15

Jesus wept.

—John 11:35

Jesus, you entered in our humanity. You ate with us, walked with us, and mourned with us. Thank you.

June 16

A fool uttereth all his mind: but a wise man keepeth it in till afterwards.

—Proverbs 29:11

I know I said something quick and foolish today! Lord, please still my tongue when it might hurt another.

June 17

Thank you for the sounds, sights, and smells of summer!
You walk with us in both times of sorrow and times of
joy—and in the summer, I find it easier to be joyful! I offer
a prayer of thanksgiving today for the beauties of your
creation, for long, sunny days, and for the gifts of rest and
relaxation. For family reunions and vacations, I thank you!

June 18

Keep me at evening,

Keep me at morning,

Keep me at noon,

I am tired,

astray and stumbling,

shield me from sin.

—Celtic Traditional

June 19

Dear God, from whom every family receives its true name, I pray for all the members of my family; for those who are growing up, that they may increase in wisdom and love; for those facing changes, that they may meet them with hope; for those who are weak, that they may find strength; for those with heavy burdens, that they may carry them lightly; for those who are old and frail, that they may grow in faith.

June 20

Thank you for the joy of young children, which acts as an example for us all. When I see a grandchild running towards her grandpa, I see love in action.

June 21

Open my eyes that I may see glimpses of truth
thou sendest me; place in my hands the wonderful key that shall unclasp, and set me free:
Silently now I wait for thee, ready, my God, thy
will to see; open my eyes, illumine me, Spirit
divine! Open my ears that I may hear voices
of truth thou sendest clear; And while the
wavenotes fall on my ear, everything false will
disappear: Silently now I wait for thee, ready
my God, thy will to see; open my heart illumine
me, spirit divine!

—Clara H. Scott

June 22

Josiah…reigned thirty and one years in Jerusalem. And he did that which was right in the sight of the Lord, and walked in all the way of David his father, and turned not aside to the right hand or to the left.

—2 Kings 22:1–2

Do I have Josiah's courage, to walk in your ways when others around me have fallen away? Please grant me courage!

June 23

Drop thy still dews of quietness, Till all our strivings cease; Take from our souls the strain and stress, And let our ordered lives confess The beauty of thy peace.

—John Greenleaf Whittier

June 24

But if the cloud were not taken up, then they
journeyed not till the day that it was taken up.

—Exodus 40:37

Let me pay attention to your cues, God, for sometimes you
guide me to action and sometimes you guide me to wait
patiently. Let me trust that the events that need to unfold
will unfold in your time, not mine.

June 25

We call you our redeemer and saviour because you redeem us from our empty, trivial existence, you save us from our foolish fears. This is your work, which you have completed and will continue to complete every moment.

—Søren Kierkegaard

June 26

For then thou shalt make thy way prosperous, and then thou shalt have good success.

—Joshua 1:8

One can seem to succeed in life by treating others badly, by turning to sin and cruelty, but that does not guarantee happiness or success. Only by following God's ways can we truly prosper in healthy ways—at work, at home, and most of all spiritually.

June 27

You must hand yourself and all your inward experiences...into the care and keeping of our God. And leave them there. He made you, He understands you, He knows how to manage you, and you must trust Him to do it.

—Hannah Whitall Smith

June 28

And he went into the synagogue, and spake boldly for the space of three months, disputing and persuading the things concerning the kingdom of God.

—Acts 19:8

Saul changed his path in life when you intervened, and became a titan of the faith. Let me always be open to change at your direction and boldness in my own faith.

June 29

I will tell you, I have heard…God has two dwellings, one in heaven and the other in the meek and thankful heart.

—Izaak Walton

June 30

Remember Abraham, Isaac, and Israel, thy servants, to whom thou swarest by thine own self, and saidst unto them, I will multiply your seed as the stars of heaven, and all this land that I have spoken of will I give unto your seed, and they shall inherit it forever.

—Exodus 32:13

God of your goodness give me yourself, for you are sufficient for me. I cannot properly ask anything less, to be worthy of you. If I were to ask less, I should always be in want. In you alone do I have all.

—Julian of Norwich

July

July 1

A new month of new chances! Let me change what needs changing and keep what needs keeping.

If I am right, Thy grace impart, still in the right to stay; if I am wrong, oh teach my heart to find that better way.

— Alexander Pope

July 2

I am not able to bear all this people alone, because it is too heavy for me.

—Numbers 11:14

God, when I am struggling, my instinct is to hide that from others. I want to be seen as having my act together. But some things are too heavy for one person to carry alone. Don't let my pride keep me from my faith community!

July 3

For when thy judgments are in the earth, the inhabitants of the world will learn righteousness.

—Isaiah 26:9

Lord, I want my children to learn and value righteousness. Will you help me model integrity and righteousness myself? Will you help me teach them?

July 4

Lord God, I have nothing to fear when I place my trust in you. You own all things. All good things for my life are in your hands to grant at the right time. Teach me to rest in the knowledge that you never withhold any good thing from those who walk with you in a spirit of uprightness.

Trust in the Lord with all thine heart; and lean not unto thine own understanding.

—Proverbs 3:5

July 5

God, I think someone I love is not being truthful with me. Please help me discern truth and forgive this person.

On a huge hill, cragged, and steep, Truth stands, and he that will reach her, about must, and about must go.

—John Donne

July 6

Finally, brethren, whatsoever things are true, whatsoever things are honest, whatsoever things are just, whatsoever things are pure, whatsoever things are lovely, whatsoever things are of good report; if there be any virtue, and if there be any praise, think on these things.

—Philippians 4:8

Let me never forget to encourage others, by seeking what is just, honest, and pure, and appreciating it where I see it!

July 7

The very word "God" suggests care, kindness, goodness; and the idea of God in his infinity is infinite care, infinite kindess, infinite goodness.

—Henry Ward Beecher

Since neediness can carry the stigma of weakness, we sometimes feel shame when we are in need. But true need is nothing to be ashamed of. God loves us, and he knows that we have deep spiritual needs that we can manage to ignore when we are physically comfortable. Our neediness, therefore, creates a meeting place for us with God, a place where we discover that we don't have to go it alone on our own strength, for God walks with us, providing for all our various needs.

July 8

Someone I love has been going through some medical tests. It might be nothing; it might be serious. The uncertainty is difficult to handle, but I'm also a little bit afraid of answers, for once they arrive we may have to transition immediately to treatment and its side effects. I pray for my loved one's health. I pray that you be a comfort. I pray that whatever may happen, there is a sense of peace. I pray that we will be obedient to your will and your plan as you lead us through this treacherous time.

July 9

O God, our help in ages past, our hope for years to come; be Thou our guide while life shall last.

—Isaac Watts

July 10

If you would have God hear you when you pray, you must hear Him when He speaks.

— Thomas Benton Brooks

In the rush of waves, in the rustling of the trees, I almost feel I can hear your voice. Deep in my heart, I do.

July 11

That ye might walk worthy of the Lord unto all pleasing, being fruitful in every good work, and increasing in the knowledge of God.

—Colossians 1:10

July 12

God, you are
my provider. I
want to look to
you to meet my
needs, whether
you meet them
supernaturally
or in ordinary
ways. Help me
see and rejoice
in your goodness
to me. Help me
not turn down
your provision
if it comes to me
through others.
I surrender my
pride and my
fear to you, as I
trust your wis-
dom for my life.
Amen.

July 13

We may run, walk, stumble, drive, or fly, but let us never lose sight of the reason for the journey, or miss a chance to see a rainbow on the way.

Lord Jesus, as I walk with you, there is no cause for fear or anxiety. Thank you for inviting me to be in this close relationship with you. I lay down the concerns of my life right now, knowing you will take care of each one in your time and in your way—the way that is best for me. Help me walk with peace in my heart and mind today as I place my hand in yours. In your name. Amen.

July 14

Blessed and praised be the Lord, from whom comes all the good that we speak and think and do.

—Teresa of Avila

July 15

Let your heart therefore by perfect with the
Lord our God, to walk in his statutes.

—1 Kings 8:61

Lord, the people of the Bible were far from perfect. But
they yearned to be made perfect by you. So do I.

July 16

And beside this, giving all diligence, add to your faith virtue; and to virtue knowledge.

—2 Peter 1:5

I don't want to stall in my faith and grow complacent, thinking that I am doing "basically okay" and therefore don't need to keep growing, changing, and deepening my relationship with you.

July 17

Lord, I need to know that you are near and that you care. When I focus on you and fix my attention on your sufficiency instead of on my needs, my fear fades and my faith rises up. I want to live in that peace today. Meet me here, I ask. In Jesus' name. Amen.

July 18

For in much wisdom is much grief: and he that increaseth knowledge increaseth sorrow.

—Ecclesiastes 1:18

As I go through this day, help me to be sensitive to the fears and cares of my fellow workers. Remind me not to add my grievances and burdens to their own.

July 19

For we are his workmanship, created in Christ
Jesus unto good works.

—Ephesians 2:10

July 20

But though he cause grief, yet will he have compassion according to the multitude of his mercies.

—Lamentations 3:32

Merciful God, I know that troubled times can draw me closer to you, for it is then that I call out to you. Please kindle in me a fire to seek you out when I am not in distress. I want to seek closeness to you whatever my mood.

July 21

That bill is due, and the money is not there. Your child is not home, and it's past the curfew. You need to make an important decision, but you have no idea what you should do. What stressful situation is staring you in the face right now? Don't be afraid to call on God. It's okay to be weak and needy; God is your strength and sufficiency. He wants to be there for you. He will come alongside you and show you the way to peace of heart and mind.

July 22

I thank you today for human ingenuity! You have created some of us to be problem solvers, Lord, to be inventors and improvers. Thank you for the gift of people who ask, "What if?"

July 23

I cannot go beyond the commandment of the
Lord, to do either good or bad of mine own
mind; but what the Lord saith, that will
I speak?

—Numbers 24:13

A friend asked for my take on a potential course of action.
I think she was hurt when I couldn't support it. Please let
me be loving while holding firm to my own beliefs.

July 24

Father, lift my eyes to see the joy of relationship with you regardless of what I cannot see right now in the way you provide for my physical needs. I rest this day in your promise that you will supply all of my needs, every single one of them, in Christ Jesus. In my neediness, you make a place for me to meet with you. Thank you for your desire to walk with me and for your power to provide. Amen.

July 25

The root of faith produces the flower of heart-joy.

—Charles Spurgeon

July 26

For as the sufferings of Christ abound in us, so our consolation also aboundeth by Christ.

—2 Corinthians 1:5

July 27

Worry, anxiety, frustration, tension, stress—these can eat us alive if we let them. But we don't need to let them if we understand that God helps us in times of trouble. God's love for his children includes his desire to carry our burdens, to give us rest in the middle of chaos, and to teach us the secret of peace in all circumstances. No matter what overwhelming situation we find ourselves in, God is still bigger. God is able to show himself strong on our behalf. Take heart today! God is with you and for you! You can find peace as you walk with him.

July 28

Because all those men which have seen my glory, and my miracles, which I did in Egypt and in the wilderness, and have tempted me now these ten times, and have not hearkened to my voice

—Number 14:22

Lord, sometimes I forget what you have done for me in the past. We humans have short memories. I call to mind the instances of your past faithfulness, and thank you again!

July 29

Father, the world is such an uncertain place. I realize that there is no real security outside of your care. That's why I'm grateful that you, the Almighty God, are the one who walks with me on this journey. I praise your name because nothing is too difficult for you.

July 30

But though he had done so many miracles before them, yet they believed not on him.

—John 12:37

Jesus, where am I unaware of your presence in my life? Where have I refused to believe that you could be at work? Where have I denied you?

July 31

Ask yourself whether you have this day done one thing because he said, Do it, or once abstained because he said, Do not do it! It is simply absurd to say you believe...if you do not do anything he tells you.

—George MacDonald

August

August 1

The great thing in this world is not so much where we stand, as in what direction we are moving: To reach the port of heaven, we must sail sometimes with the wind and sometimes against it—but we must sail, and not drift, nor lie at anchor.

—Oliver Wendell Holmes

August 2

At the point where we become completely powerless to help ourselves, we are forced to surrender our lives to God's control. What happens from there is totally his call. And if we are uncertain of God's concern for us, it can be a scary thing. But the truth about God is that he is good, and he is willing and able to rescue us in our helplessness and to keep us safe from harm. His deepest desire, though, is to continue walking with us after the crisis has passed, guiding us and keeping us day by day so that we need never face those times of helplessness without him.

August 3

Hold fast to the Bible as the sheet anchor of your liberties. Write its precepts in your hearts, and practice them in your lives.

—Ulysses Grant

August 4

Lord Jesus, I'm
thankful that
you watch over
my life. When
I have no place
to turn for help,
I have you. I al-
ways have you.
And you are
the best place
to turn for help.
Thank you for
hearing my cries
and for rescuing
me. What would
I do without
you? You are the
one who saves.

August 5

The day was long, the burden I had borne
seemed heavier that I could no longer bear;
And then it lifted—but I did not know
someone had knelt in prayer. Had taken me to
God that very hour, and asked the easing of the
load, and he in infinite compassion, had stooped
down and lifted the burden from me. We cannot
tell how often as we pray for some bewildered
one, hurt and distressed, the answer comes, but
many times these hearts find sudden peace and
rest. Someone had prayed, and faith, a lifted
hand reached up to God, and he reached down
that day. So many, many hearts have need of
prayer— Then, let us, let us pray.

—Anonymous

August 6

For ye have need of patience, that, after ye have done the will of God, ye might receive the promise.

—Hebrews 10:36

Patience is power; with time and patience, the mulberry leaf becomes silk.

August 7

If any of you lack wisdom, let him ask of God, that giveth to all men liberally, and upbraideth not; and it shall be given him.

—James 1:5

I have a wise, thoughtful friend. When I bring problems to her, she listens with compassion, and she always has some unexpected insight. She uses her spiritual gifts for good!

August 8

There is no fear in love; but perfect love casteth out fear: because fear hath torment. He that feareth is not made perfect in love.

— 1 John 4:18

I try to cling to your love, but fear creeps in around the edges. I ask you to banish it, to deepen my trust.

August 9

Begin to weave and God will give the thread.

—German proverb

August 10

Him that is weak in the faith receive ye, but not to doubtful disputations.

—Romans 14:1

When I am weak and stumble, you give me sympathy instead of sermons. You show me mercy instead of meanness. You speak tenderly instead of tearing down my already-fragile ego. You are a true friend.

August 11

But thou shalt love thy neighbour as thyself: I am the Lord.

—Leviticus 19:18

The love of a friend has often seemed like my life preserver, keeping me afloat in turbulent waters.

August 12

True friendship is a knot that angel hands
have tied.

— Anonymous

August 13

The Lord shall fight for you, and ye shall hold your peace.

—Exodus 14:14

Lord, you stand near my side during my greatest struggles. You deliver me from all my fears.

August 14

Joy is perfect acquiescence in God's will because the soul delights in God himself.

—H.W. Webb-Peploe

August 15

Hope melts the frost from the tiniest leaf, allowing it to grow stronger in the healing light of the sun.

August 16

Father, I love that you call me your child. It helps me see the true nature of my relationship with you. I need you in so many ways. When I'm helpless, teach me not to feel ashamed…just as children who have loving and attentive parents are not ashamed of asking for what they need. I confess my helplessness today as a gift from you that allows me to experience your strong and capable parental love for me.

Seated on an outcropping of rock high above the snow-bound valley, my eye is drawn to the evergreen, and hope stirs within my breast. Thank you, God.

August 18

Do not look back and agonize over roads not taken, dreams not pursued. Instead, look ahead to the future to new roads to discover and new dreams to fulfill.

August 19

Treasured memories form a basis for today's choices, and by using faith's discernment, I've learned what matters and what lasts.

August 20

A wise mind knows that adverse events are blessed opportunities for growth in disguise. Thank you for setbacks!

August 21

I have fought a good fight, I have finished my course, I have kept the faith.

—2 Timothy 4:7

Faith is my soul's good friend that urges me on, convincing me I will victoriously reach the finish line in this race called my life.

Heavenly Father, I'm grateful that you see my helplessness, and you move in quickly to help me whenever I call on you. Forgive me for the times my pride has gotten in the way of receiving the help you offer me. Cause me to become more confident that you want to help me. I praise you for showing me that in my helplessness, I never walk alone, for you are my rescuer, my hero. Amen.

August 23

Have we trials and temptations?
Is there trouble anywhere?
We should never be discouraged,
Take it to the Lord in prayer.
Can we find a friend so faithful
Who will all our sorrows share?
Jesus knows our every weakness,
take it to the Lord in prayer.

—Joseph M. Scriven,
"What a Friend We Have in Jesus"

August 24

Teach me to feel another's woe, to hide the fault
I see; that mercy I to others show, that mercy
show to me.

— Alexander Pope

August 25

The past, O God of yesterdays, todays, and promise-filled tomorrows, can be an anchor or a launching pad. It's sometimes so easy to look back on the pain and hurt and believe the future may be an instant replay. Help us to accept the aches of the past and put them in perspective so we can also see the many ways you supported and nurtured us. Then, believing in your promise of regeneration, launch us into the future free and excited to live in joy.

August 26

Lord, give me faith that tries and tests the things unseen, and assures itself of thee who art the truth, that doubt may not overwhelm, nor darkness cover me; give me hope, that I may follow the light of thy sure promises, and lose not the way nor fall into byways; give me love, that I may give thee myself as thou givest; for thou, O Lord God, are the thing that I long for; and thou art blessedness beyond all thought and heart's desiring.

— Frederick Macnutt

August 27

For I have said, Mercy shall be built up for ever: thy faithfulness shalt thou establish in the very heavens.

—Psalm 89:2

Faith is like a tiny seed of belief inside us that grows into a mighty tree, each leaf a new direction, each branch a new opportunity.

August 28

Life with faith has meaning and purpose. It transforms the smallest actions into elements of significance, contributing to a better world.

August 29

From each of life's misfortunes, large or small, comes a new beginning, an opportunity to renew your faith in the future.

August 30

Thank you for this last bit of summer before we move into fall. We need to buckle down to schoolwork and all the things we've been putting off for vacation and recreation. Thank you both for reinvigorating rest and for work!

August 31

Take a moment to contemplate how big the world is and how fragile our bodies are. What a miracle that we are able to move about in such a world and survive one day in it! It would seem that we are far more helpless than we often realize and that God is far more involved in taking care of us than we may be able to comprehend. In humility and love he works behind the scenes in our lives, granting us tremendous help and provision. These gifts are worthy of our ongoing thanks and praise, because he has not left us to walk alone in this world.

September

September 1

Dear Lord,

In this time of back-to-school excitement, I pray for all students who are returning to the classroom. May they have a productive year of education and friendship. Please grant teachers patience and fulfillment, and bless all maintenance workers, administrators, principals, and aides who work behind the scenes. I pray especially for those who are apprehensive about this return—non-traditional learners, children who are being bullied, and children and staff who are dealing with weighty issues at home. May they feel a sense of your presence as they walk into the school each day.

September 2

Watch a child conquer his world. Curiosity over a faraway object leads to walking. The need to voice an opinion leads to speaking. Dear God, let me allow myself to be a child again, discovering and accomplishing new things. When things seem a little out of reach, help us to stretch to meet them!

September 3

The righteous shall flourish like the palm tree:
he shall grow like a cedar in Lebanon.

—Psalm 92:12

Lord, draw me to your Word! Give me a thirst for righteousness. I want to grow according to your ways, seeking your path instead of following my own. I want to choose to walk with you, each and every day.

September 4

And it came to pass, that, while they communed together and reasoned, Jesus himself drew near, and went with them.

—Luke 24:15

Father God,

You send us companions on our journey to you—we walk this path with all those who seek you. Like Cleopas and his companion on the road to Emmaus, we talk together, share our stories, and try to discern the presence of Jesus in our lives. Thank you for those you send to be spiritual support!

September 5

Come walk with me through life, my friend,
arm in arm we'll stroll.
With love and hope to light our path,
and faith to guide our souls.

September 6

Give us this day our daily bread.

—Matthew 6:11

Thank you for sustaining food, from plain oatmeal for everyday breakfasts to exquisite chocolates for special occasions. Thank you for shared meals with family and friends, where we also share what's going on in our lives. Whatever we eat, ultimately it is your love for us that sustains us.

September 7

My soul thirsteth for God, for the living God.

—Psalm 42:2

How can I be lonely in a crowd? But sometimes I am. Let me see those feelings of loneliness and restlessness not as bad things that I must try to escape, Father God, but as sensations that lead me to retreat and seek your presence. You are my peace and my hope, and only in you can I find rest.

September 8

Understanding is the reward of faith. So do not seek to understand in order to believe, but believe so that you may understand.

—Saint Augustine

September 9

We teach children that the Sun, the Moon, and the stars
are always in the sky, even when we cannot see them. Let
me trust, Lord, that even when I don't perceive you working in my life, you are still present!

September 10

There was a man in Jerusalem, whose name was
Simeon; and the same man was just and devout,
waiting for the consolation of Israel: and the
Holy Ghost was upon him.

—Luke 2:25

Thank you for our elders, those grandparents and great-
aunts and uncles who have modeled faith and generosity
to us! Thank you for those stalwart members of our faith
community who, like Anna and Simeon, have grown deep
in their faith over their long lives, acting as a beacon to us.

September 11

When peace, like a river, attendeth my way.
When sorrows like sea billows roll;
Whatever my lot, thou hast taught me to say,
It is well, it is well with my soul.
It is well with my soul, it is well,
it is well with my soul.

—Horatio G. Spafford

September 12

Lord, you know I have been dealing with someone with a difficult personality. Whatever our issues, help me be charitable in my thoughts and words. Please extend your grace over both of us, and send your Holy Spirit to inspire us both to kindness. Please help me remember that you want this person to be loving and whole in you, not isolated and alone. Please grant us a way to walk in harmony with you and each other.

September 13

Seeing my children grow more independent is tremendously rewarding, but sometimes it brings a bit of sadness too, as they naturally spend more time with their friends and studies and hobbies. Father, please give me a generous and encouraging heart. Let me support their independence even as I provide a safe haven for them to return to when they run into problems and need some advice or just a listening ear.

September 14

And I will walk among you, and will be your God, and ye shall be my people.

—Leviticus 26:12

How amazing you are, O Lord! You are all-powerful and all-knowing, and yet you promise to walk with me. You sent Jesus, your son, to live as one of us, to walk among us. You claim us as your own. When I am feeling downcast, let me remember that the Lord of the universe chooses to love me. Thank you and praise you!

September 15

Fall is a time of change. Sometimes that change is beautiful, as when the leaves begin to change color. Sometimes that change brings loss, as the days grow shorter and the trees grow bare. Let me never be afraid to change and grow myself—and let me remember that you are with me even in times of loss and sorrow.

September 16

If there be anywhere on earth [where] a lover of God is always kept safe from falling, I know nothing of it, for it was not shown to me. But this was shown: that in falling and rising again we are always kept in the same precious love.

—Julian of Norwich

September 17

Be still, and know that I am God.

—Psalm 46:10

Today, I feel empty—drained of love. It's time to still my heart and open it up to receive all the love that's being offered to me. Thank you, God, for the gift of yourself and your love.

September 18

When my spouse and I are arguing, let me believe that love will find a way to bridge this chasm between us. Let me hold on to memories of lovely, loving days we have enjoyed, and let me look forward and believe we will have more of them. Lord, I know that you brought my spouse and I together. Let me trust that you will guide us in a path forward whenever we go through thorny times.

September 19

Today I thank you for medical professionals: doctors and nurses and technicians. I ask you to bless them, to give them the gift of being compassionate with their patients, to help them say the right words when breaking bad news. I ask you to protect and shield them from burnout, that they have the support they need in their own lives to heal from the difficult times they go through. Please help them know that you are always with them, Our Great Physician.

September 20

And moreover, because the preacher was wise, he still taught the people knowledge; yea, he gave good heed, and sought out, and set in order many proverbs. The preacher sought to find out acceptable words: and that which was written was upright, even words of truth.

—Ecclesiastes 12:9–10

Father God, please bless our preachers, our pastors and church leaders. Please give them wise counsel to share with us your words of truth and life. Please keep them strong in their own faith as they foster ours.

September 21

And when Peter was come down out of the
ship, he walked on the water, to go to Jesus.
But when he saw the wind boisterous, he was
afraid; and beginning to sink, he cried, saying,
Lord, save me.

—Matthew 14:29–30

Jesus, sometimes I see your presence so clearly in my life,
and it is easy to walk towards you. But then I lose my focus
and take my eyes off you, and begin to sink back into old
habits and old sins. During those times when I cannot walk
towards you in confidence, let me cry out, like Peter, for
you to save me.

September 22

Jesus, a friend was sharp-tongued and impatient with me recently. I know she's going through some things in her own life, but it smarted! Since it's not like her, do I just let it go? Do I bring it up with her so we can talk it through? Please guide my actions and show me a path forward. Most of all, let me forgive her truly, as you forgive me.

September 23

How marvelous our bodies! May we care for them today
with all the reverence and honor we might extend toward
any great gift that defies explanation.

For he shall give his angels charge over thee, to keep thee in all thy ways.

—Psalm 91:11

In heaven, the angelic choir sings, and a bright hosanna of music flows and swells throughout the Holy City. It is the perfect beginning to an endless day. I thank you for your angels, Lord, who guard me daily and walk with me. And with the angels, I give thanks to you, our Creator!

September 25

When illness strikes, the effects go beyond the physical suffering. Fear, despair, and terrible isolation arise as the illness prolongs itself. It feels natural to lash out at your failing body, medicine that does not help, and even at the God who allowed this terrible thing to happen to you. The fate of the patient's loved ones can be equally painful, as they stand by feeling helpless to be of any real assistance. Yet, be assured that the Lord is there among you.

September 26

No matter how deep a rut we dig ourselves into, the arms of God are long enough to lift us up into a newer life free from struggle. No matter how dark a tunnel we crawl into, the love of God is strong enough to reach in and guide us toward a brighter life, free from fear.

September 27

We love him, because he first loved us.

—1 John 4:19

Lord, thank you for heirlooms. The rocking chair where
I remember sitting on Grandma's lap, and then rocking
my own child, is now being passed down. I cherish the
thought of every moment I will hold my own grandchild.
I thank you for all these connections to the past and these
legacies of love, for all love flows ultimately from you.

September 28

Forgiveness is the central virtue in God's treasure chest—God's forgiveness of us and our forgiveness of others and ourselves. At times we find that forgiveness comes very easily, even for grievous and painful hurts. But many times, we seem powerless to forgive, no matter how hard we try. This is when God's forgiving grace has the opportunity to touch and change us and then be extended to others through our example.

September 29

Fear ye not therefore, ye are of more value than many sparrows.

—Matthew 10:31

Lord, you know I'm a little worried about finances this month. Please help me trust in you, that we'll get through this rough patch. Ease my fears and let me be happy for those ways in which I have enough. And help me never forget to be generous to others.

September 30

If you pray truly, you will feel within yourself a great assurance, and the angels will be your companions.

—Evagrius of Pontus

October

October 1

I look at this month's calendar and see how many things I'm already committed to do! Dear Lord, please guide me through all my endeavors during this coming month. Please let me be a witness to your love by being loving myself, with everyone I encounter, whether strangers or family or friends or colleagues. And let me be mindful that I spend time with you, that I not make myself so busy that I forget to sit in quiet prayer each day.

October 2

Creator of all, I hold up to you our aging pet. She's still enjoying life, but she's slowing down, and we know we will face some difficult decisions soon. Please let us appreciate the time we have, and not prolong any pain.

October 3

Come now, and let us reason together, saith the
Lord: though your sins be as scarlet, they shall
be as white as snow; though they be red like
crimson, they shall be as wool.

—Isaiah 1:18

On laundry day, as I'm removing stains that have been
allowed to set, I remember this verse. Thank you for the
power of your forgiveness. Please let me turn to you in re-
pentance as soon as I've done something wrong, not allowing that sin to set and deepen and become habitual.

October 4

Whither shall I go from thy spirit? or whither shall I flee from thy presence?

— Psalm 139:7

Lord, you know me. Sometimes, that thought is intimidating. I don't want you to see all my flaws and foibles! I become discouraged by the thought of how petty I must seem to you, how earthly my concerns. I think that if you truly know me, you'll think me unworthy of your love.

But I know you do love me! You alone can both fully know me and fully love me. I thank you for that incredible gift.

October 5

For nature around me, I thank you.

For grass and tree, I thank you.

For sun and rain, I thank you.

For fields of grain, I thank you.

For cloudy skies, I thank you.

For mountain highs, I thank you.

For desert flowers, I thank you.

For twilight hours, I thank you.

October 6

There's an old joke that it's easy to love your neighbor in church, but it gets much harder in the church parking lot! Lord, I'd like to ask you to be with me today and every day when I spend time in transit. Whether I'm dealing with rude drivers or inconsiderate fellow commuters, let me be loving and forgiving, and dial down the road rage—or even just the "road irritation."

October 7

Where there is charity and wisdom,
there is neither fear nor ignorance.
Where there is patience and humility,
there is neither anger nor vexation.
Where there is poverty and joy,
there is neither greed nor avarice.
Where there is peace and meditation,
there is neither anxiety nor doubt.

—Saint Francis of Assisi

October 8

For thou hast possessed my reins: thou hast covered me in my mother's womb.

—Psalm 139:13

I offer up prayers today for all expectant parents. Keep mother and child healthy. Ease any anxieties to make this a time of anticipation instead of fear. What joy the promise of new life brings!

October 9

We live in an age of technological wonders! How amazing it is to be able to connect with old friends and distant cousins from hundreds of miles away. Let me use technology to make my circle of love wider, to bring your love to more people. Let me be warm and inviting in a way that conveys your love and points people towards you.

October 10

Lord,

Send me an angel to guide me and guard me, to lead and direct me, to comfort and hold me.

Send me an angel who knows what my heart needs most and who always has the highest and best solutions to my most challenging problems.

Send me an angel to walk with me through the dark and hold my hand as I tread the rocky road of life.

Send me an angel soon, Lord.

Amen

October 11

How about some help around the house, Lord, where I need your guidance to make homemaking a shared endeavor rather than Mom's Motel? Inspire me with plans to enlist instead of accuse. I'm counting on you to be at the dinner-discussion table and in the kitchen afterward with the new cleanup crew. Time for a shift change.

October 12

Lord, I am grateful that you don't have a list of criteria for being eligible for salvation. What insecurity that would create in us! I feel blessed that I don't need to resort to servile fear or self-important boasting when it comes to my standing with you. Your salvation is a gift available to all and secured by your merits (not mine). It is received only by grace through faith in you.

October 13

Ask, and it shall be given you; seek, and ye shall find; knock, and it shall be opened unto you.

—Matthew 7:7

Life has made the most hopeful among us skeptical, Lord of truth. Much is bogus, and we are uncertain. Thank you for the gift of doubt, for it sparks our seeking. Keep us lively and excited as we set off on quests blessed by you, heeding your advice to knock, seek, ask.

To every thing there is a season, and a time to
every purpose under the heaven:
A time to be born, and a time to die;
a time to plant, and a time to pluck up that
which is planted;
A time to kill, and a time to heal; a time to
break down, and a time to build up;
A time to weep, and a time to laugh; a time to
mourn, and a time to dance;
A time to cast away stones, and a time to gather
stones together; a time to embrace, and a time to
refrain from embracing;
A time to get, and a time to lose; a time to keep,
and a time to cast away;
A time to rend, and a time to sew; a time to keep
silence, and a time to speak;
A time to love, and a time to hate; a time of war,
and a time of peace.

—Ecclesiastes 3:1–8

October 15

He hath made every thing beautiful in his time:
also he hath set the world in their heart, so that
no man can find out the work that God maketh
from the beginning to the end.

—Ecclesiastes 3:11

Lord, how awesome you are, and how incredible your
works. Every time I go hiking, I see something just a little
bit different. No sunset or sunrise is the same. You continue your work of joyful creation every day!

October 16

For I was an hungred, and ye gave me meat: I was thirsty, and ye gave me drink: I was a stranger, and ye took me in.

—Matthew 25:35

How can we recognize any of your needful ones we are to feed, clothe, and tend, Lord, when we see menace in every outstretched hand? Inspire and help us reclaim our world for living in, not hiding from. Let me not fear strangers.

October 17

Let your peace rest upon our home, dear God. We do not know how to love one another as you have loved us. We fail to reach out the way you have gathered us in. We forget how to give when only taking fills our minds. And, most of all, we need your presence to know we are more than just parents and children. We are always your beloved sons and daughters here. Let your peace rest upon our home, dear God.

October 18

Truth is a narrow road, and it's easy to fall to one side or the other. For every beautiful kernel of truth, there are a thousand lies that can be made around it. Staying on the straight-and-narrow would be impossible if it weren't for the Spirit of God, who leads us to all truth. Delving into God's Word with the Holy Spirit to guide us is the best way to stay on track and keep walking in the truth.

Therefore will I offer in his tabernacle sacrifices of joy; I will sing, yea, I will sing praises unto the Lord.

—Psalm 27:6

Today I want to praise your name, God. I want to be joyful in a way that spills over, full of awe and thanksgiving. I want to make a sacrifice of praise, to revel in the works of your hands, to delight in your awesome power.

October 20

I ask your blessings today on those who may feel alone and lonely: the ill, the housebound, those in nursing homes, the newly divorced. I ask that they feel a sense of your consoling presence. I ask that those who interact with them be moved with a spirit of kindness. Please instill in me that same spirit of kindness, that I will recognize loneliness and be willing to walk with those who are experiencing it!

October 21

O for a closer walk with God,
a calm and heav'nly frame,
a light to shine upon the road
that leads me to the Lamb!

Where is the blessedness I knew
when first I sought the Lord?
Where is the soul refreshing view
of Jesus and His Word?

— William Cowper,
"O! for a Closer Walk with God"

October 22

He hath shewed thee, O man, what is good; and
what doth the Lord require of thee, but to do
justly, and to love mercy, and to walk humbly
with thy God?

—Micah 6:8

Step by step, I walk towards you, O Lord. Even though I
know the way, sometimes my steps falter. Please put in my
heart the desire to do good and to walk with you.

October 23

It's the time of year when we like stews and soups and chili, meals prepared in the slow cooker, where our house smells warm and cozy. Thank you, Lord, for the blessings of this time of year, for warm drinks on crisp days, for the memories of picking apples, for all the joy we see around us.

October 24

It is of the Lord's mercies that we are not consumed, because his compassions fail not. They are new every morning: great is thy faithfulness.

—Lamentations 3:22–23

Let me wake up each morning determined to see your presence in my life. Let me focus throughout the day not on what I don't have, but the blessings you give me so abundantly. It's easy for me to become distracted from your presence during the course of the day—but when I look, I see your mercy and compassion at work in my life.

October 25

The king shall joy in thy strength, O Lord; and
in thy salvation how greatly shall he rejoice!

—Psalm 21:1

Sometimes a stranger smiles at me in passing, and it is a
beautiful, joy-filled, light-giving smile. It makes me want
to know their secret to happiness! I think their secret is
probably you, O Lord. Please let me be so happy in your
presence that I radiate your warmth and love even to those
who are strangers.

October 26

Sometimes when I am going through a hard time, I have friends or family members who are willing to offer help, to share my burden for a while, but I have a hard time accepting their help because I feel I should be strong and handle it alone. Father God, please help me balance independence and community. Please help me remember that part of being in a loving relationship is accepting love—that in accepting love, I accept you more deeply in my life, for you are love!

October 27

I need to ask someone for forgiveness. Part of me wants to brush off and minimize what I did, to say that what I did wasn't so bad—maybe the other person didn't even notice! But I don't want to start to walk astray in little things. God, give me strength to do this properly and offer a genuine, loving apology.

October 28

When we walk with the Lord in the light of his word, what a glory he sheds on our way! While we do his good will, he abides with us still, and with all who will trust and obey.

— John Sammis

October 29

Though he were a Son, yet learned he obedience by the things which he suffered.

—Hebrews 5:8

Obedience is a tricky concept. We don't hear as much about it in these modern days! We prize leadership, sometimes at the expense of being a good team members. When I am in a group, at work or at church or at a hobby, help me not value leadership so much that I don't appreciate the work every team member does. And when I am in a leadership role, help me remember to be obedient to your will and your words. Let me follow the model of Jesus.

October 30

Oh Deliverer of Peace, you sent Christ to us not as a warrior, not as a judge, not as an enforcer, but as a baby, a healer, a teacher. Help me to follow Christ's example as peacekeeper in my home. Help me instill in my children the ways of peace by acting peaceful not punishing, problem-solving not judging, cooperating not coercing. Help me to show my children your peace so that they may bring peace to others.

October 31

Lord, a friend is going through an incredibly difficult time. Sometimes even well-meaning words can grate on raw nerves, and I don't want to say the wrong thing or, in trying to make things better, minimize her pain. When I am with her, please give me the right words to say at the right time—whether they are words of encouragement, commiseration, or understanding. And if what she needs is simply a comforting hug while she cries, let me be present to her. Sometimes silence is the best gift we have to offer.

November

November 1

Lord, we praise you for all the beauty and wonder you've placed in the world. How creative of you to think of a creature as exuberant and joyful as the hummingbird! How interesting that you sprinkled spots on the backs of the newborn fawns that follow along behind their mother through our backyard. Let us never become so accustomed to your glorious creation that we take it for granted, Lord. You've blessed us with a wonderland, and we thank you for it.

November 2

God, if I were to boil down all the good news in the universe and look to see what I'd ended up with, there would be the eternal realities of your goodness, your love, and your faithfulness. And in this world, I don't have to look far for them—family, food, shelter, clothing, seasons, tides, sun, moon, stars, life, beauty, truth, salvation. And that's just a sampling, a preview of a much longer list. I'm moved to praise you and to tell you how much I love you back.

November 3

Take this burden from me, Lord,
Free me from this pain.
Let me move with ease and grace
And walk in health again.
Take this yoke upon you, Lord,
And help me toward my goal,
I'm tired of being sick and tired
And long to be made whole.
Release me from my illness
And restore me to my best.
If you can do that for me, Lord,
I'll take care of the rest.

November 4

Lord, when I see anger and strife around me, it's difficult to keep my own equilibrium and trust in you. I try to have faith that "all things work together for good to them that love God" (Romans 8:28), but my faith does falter. When I'm surrounded by division, let me be rooted in faith, unshaken by the passing concerns of this world. Let me be a person of peace myself—not false peace, that ignores problems that need to be addressed—but the true peace that comes from you.

November 5

But the fruit of the Spirit is love, joy, peace, longsuffering, gentleness, goodness, faith, meekness, temperance: against such there is no law.

—Galatians 5:22–23

When I feel alone or lonely, sometimes the best remedy is to do something for someone else—to love God by loving my neighbor! It's so easy to get tangled up in my own isolating concerns. God, please produce good fruit in me. Let me seek your Spirit and practice these virtues.

November 6

Hope blooms like a beautiful rose amidst the thorns of life. Hope knows that in the midst of feeling all alone, God is still with you. When you feel hopeless, instead of searching for hope, seek God. You will find that hope will be your constant companion when you do.

The angel of the Lord encampeth round about
them that fear him, and delivereth them.

—Psalm 34:7

Angels look for the best in us and then they nourish that
place. They see a vision of whom God has created us to be
and they dream that dream with us.

November 8

And as he lay and slept under a juniper tree, behold, then an angel touched him, and said unto him, Arise and eat.

— 1 Kings 19:5

When Elijah was feeling deep despair, an angel came to him and urged him to eat. Elijah ate and slept before he resumed his journey. When I am feeling mired in problems, Lord, please remind me to take a step back, to eat and sleep and breathe, before tackling the obstacle in front of me. Let me always remember that you are the one that gives me sustaining life.

November 9

But as for me, I will come into thy house in the multitude of thy mercy: and in thy fear will I worship toward thy holy temple.

—Psalm 5:7

Mercy is not something we need beg of you, O God, for your pleasure is to love us. Mercy, grace, and love are always available to us, Lord, for you are always available to us.

November 10

How grateful we are, God of Knowledge, that you created us so curious. In your wisdom, it is the searcher turning over every leaf who finds four-leaf clovers; the doubter who invents; and the determined, like a duckling pecking its way from the shell, who emerges strong enough to fly.

November 11

O Master, let me walk with thee
In lowly paths of service free;
Tell me thy secret, help me bear
The strain of toil, the fret of care.

Help me the slow of heart to move
By some clear, winning word of love;
Teach me the wayward feet to stay,
And guide them in the homeward way.

— Washington Gladden

November 12

The life which I now live in the flesh I live by the faith of the Son of God, who loved me, and gave himself for me.

—Galatians 2:20

God gives us faith as a means of getting in touch with his love. For once we have that love, we can pass it on to others.

November 13

For he hath not despised nor abhorred the affliction of the afflicted; neither hath he hid his face from him; but when he cried unto him, he heard.

—Psalm 22:24

When I am feeling uncertain and alone, I can turn to the Scriptures. The prophets often felt unworthy of their call. Hannah felt alone in her barrenness. Jesus himself cried out on the cross, quoting Psalm 22, asking why God had forsaken him. But God's love reached all of them.

November 14

God's love does not draw lines. It comes with open eyes, open arms, and an open heart. Can we take the risk of loving our neighbor with God's kind of love? It might demand more of us than we first expect.

We are naturally drawn to beautiful, kind, loving people. Mature love knows how to love those who seem unlovable, those who seem incapable of giving us anything in return for our love. This kind of love is heaven's love.

November 15

Rather than proudly striving to get ahead on our own, we must learn to relax in the provision God has made for us. Only this will bring us God's peaceful rest.

A faithful man shall abound with blessings:
but he that maketh haste to be rich shall not be
innocent.

—Proverbs 28:20

Faith thrives when we stay focused on God rather than on
ourselves. Some people blame their lack of faith on their
different circumstances. Yet rough situations are often the
catalyst for displays of great faith.

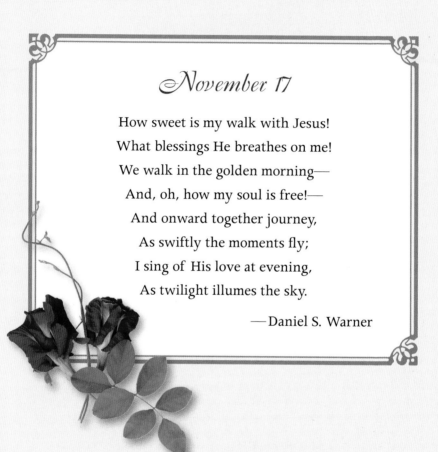

November 17

How sweet is my walk with Jesus!
What blessings He breathes on me!
We walk in the golden morning—
And, oh, how my soul is free!—
And onward together journey,
As swiftly the moments fly;
I sing of His love at evening,
As twilight illumes the sky.

—Daniel S. Warner

November 18

It takes faith to go beyond what others know—to explore new ideas, to stand on our convictions that there is something more, and to trust that God has called us to discover it.

November 19

And the very God of peace sanctify you wholly; and I pray God your whole spirit and soul and body be preserved blameless unto the coming of our Lord Jesus Christ.

— 1 Thessalonians 5:23

We all make plans for our lives and have an agenda we want to hold on to. Yet if we let go and let God be in charge, the result will bring us peace.

November 20

Only when we trust God, do we have peace and assurance in the shelter of his care. Spiritual maturity is facing each new day with patience, confident that God is in control.

November 21

Thanksgiving is almost here, and Advent and Christmas will follow! Lord, during this season let me stay focused on you. Let me be truly thankful for my blessings, and not so intent on throwing the perfect party or preparing the best meal that I forget to be kind to my family and friends. Thank you for the gifts of faith, family, and friends!

November 22

Let me seek the goodness that only God can put in my heart. If I choose to act on even one opportunity to do good, I will have introduced a new blessing into my world.

November 23

The day is thine, the night also is thine: thou hast prepared the light and the sun.

—Psalm 74:16

Just as our bodies absorb the warmth of the sun, our souls absorb the warmth of God's love.

November 24

It isn't necessary to pray in order for God to know what's on our minds—he already knows. We pray so we will know what's on God's mind. God, please share your wisdom and love with me today.

November 25

Sometimes the smallest gesture can mean so much. I thank you today, Lord, for the smile from a stranger, for the grandchild who wants to share a cookie, for the friend who reached out "just because." I thank you for the colleague who paid a compliment on a new haircut, the spouse who emptied the dishwasher when it was my turn, the teenaged rebel who gave me a hug.

November 26

Bless our little ones today;
Bid your angels close to stay.
Protect them, Lord, as all the while
We see you in each sweet smile.

November 27

Soon we'll reach the shining river,
Soon our pilgrimage will cease,
Soon our happy hearts will quiver
With the melody of peace.

Yes, we'll gather at the river,
The beautiful, the beautiful river –
Gather with the saints at the river
That flows by the throne of God.

November 28

Thy statutes have been my songs in the house
of my pilgrimage.

—Psalm 119:54

In days of old, people would travel long distances to make
pilgrimages. Let me turn my daily life into a pilgrimage
towards you, Lord. As I hike a trail, or drive to the grocery
store, or take a train to visit my child at college, let me be
mindful that I continue traveling towards you. Let me never forget that, wherever my earthly journeys take me, you
are my goal and my ultimate destination!

November 29

Casting all your care upon him; for he careth
for you.

—1 Peter 5:7

Instead of lugging around our cares, we can pray. Prayer
opens the door to peace, and every silent prayer is heard
in heaven.

November 30

I know that faith is what keeps me moving forward.
But sometimes, too, my trust allows a leisure like this.
For you, God, are the one who upholds all things.
Even as I sit here in stillness,
your breath keeps me breathing,
your mind keeps me thinking,
your love keeps me yearning for home.

December

December 1

And Mary said, Behold the handmaid of the
Lord; be it unto me according to thy word.

—Luke 1:38

As we enter the month that leads to your birth, Jesus, let
me open my heart to you as your mother did. Mary didn't
know what would happen, but she chose to follow God's
plan. What an amazing woman of faith! I see echoes of her
faith in some of the people I know from church, wise men
and women who have a sense of inner peace about them.
I know I want to be like that: let me start by saying yes to
your plan for me today.

December 2

And it came to pass, that, when Elisabeth heard the salutation of Mary, the babe leaped in her womb; and Elisabeth was filled with the Holy Ghost.

—Luke 1:41

Mary and her cousin turned to each other for support during life-changing events. They sought to help and encourage each other. When I am feeling overwhelmed and unsure, let me reach out—to seek advice, but also to celebrate with others in their own milestones.

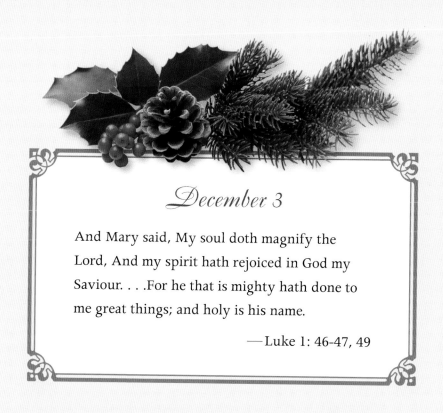

December 3

And Mary said, My soul doth magnify the
Lord, And my spirit hath rejoiced in God my
Saviour. . . .For he that is mighty hath done to
me great things; and holy is his name.

—Luke 1: 46-47, 49

When she speaks to Elizabeth, Mary praises God both for
what he has done for her and what he has done for his
people. God's plan for us is only one facet of God's larger plans. Sometimes when I have a hard time seeing God
working in my life, I can see God working in other people's
lives—and that is something to celebrate and can renew
my faith!

December 4

The Lord has promised good to me, his word my hope secures; he will my shield and portion be as long as life endures.

— John Newton

December 5

As the days grow colder and darker, I ask your blessing on those who suffer from the cold: the homeless, those whose furnace went out at the worst time, those who are struggling to pay the heating bill. Please keep them safe, and please motivate the rest of us to help in some way.

December 6

Lord, sometimes I find myself upset about minor things. I have an idea in mind about how things should be, and some-one else does not cooperate because they have their own preferences for how to do things...help me let go of the need for control. Let me especially have the wisdom to discern when I should be guiding my children, and when I should let them make their own plans and decisions, even when I think I know a better way.

December 7

Great peace have they which love thy law: and nothing shall offend them.

—Psalm 119:165

Your Word and your strictures give structure to my life. Sometimes I rebel against them, but I know that I am happier and have better relationships with others when I follow the path you have laid out for me.

December 8

My God is an awesome God, for he not only loves me, he empowers me to strive to be the best I can be every day. I am always provided with new opportunities to shine, as long as I hold fast to my faith in him, and listen for his guidance.

December 9

If any man among you seem to be religious, and
bridleth not his tongue, but deceiveth his own
heart, this man's religion is vain.

—James 1:26

As parties for Christmas and New Year's ramp up, please
help me refrain from gossip. Seeing people I haven't seen
for a while, I find that the line between catching up and
gossip can be a fine one. It's a temporary pleasure that
makes things easier in the moment, seeming to bring me
closer to the people with whom I'm talking, but it's corro-
sive over the long term.

December 10

We spend so much time shopping and decorating! It seems small, but God, please do help me choose good gifts for my family and friends, thoughtful ones that express my love for them. But please also don't let my ego get wrapped up in it, forgetting that the connection we share is more important than any individual gift. Let me stay focused on love this season, as always: your love for us, our love for you, and our love for each other.

December 11

And let the beauty of the Lord our God be upon us: and establish thou the work of our hands upon us; yea, the work of our hands establish thou it.

—Psalm 90:17

I pray today for people who work in jobs where they help others: teachers, firefighters, EMTs, librarians, caregivers, medical staff, and all others. So many go above and beyond their official duties when they see someone in need. Please keep them safe from burnout. Please give those who interact with them a thankful heart.

December 12

The heart of the prudent getteth knowledge;
and the ear of the wise seeketh knowledge.

—Proverbs 18:15

I ask your blessing on all students today, as they wrap up their semester, taking finals and finalizing projects. Please keep safe in their travels all those college students coming home, and help them have a good leave. It can be tricky for families to navigate old patterns and new changes.

December 13

For unto us a child is born, unto us a son is
given: and the government shall be upon his
shoulder: and his name shall be called Wonderful, Counsellor, The mighty God, The everlasting Father, The Prince of Peace.

—Isaiah 9:6

Jesus, you are at once awe-inspiring and a friend. Your
words bring both challenging truth and peaceful comfort.
As I look forward to your birth this advent, I think of the
innocent baby born in a manger, the man who died for us,
and the miracle of your resurrection.

December 14

Aging can be so hard, and seem so cruel. Watching parents grow more frail, feeling more aches and pains myself, I reach out to you, O Lord. This time of year brings up nostalgic memories, and it's easy to think of happier days and compare them to struggles now. Please let me see your guiding hand leading us through every life transition.

December 15

My heart is glad, and my glory rejoiceth: my flesh also shall rest in hope.

—Psalm 16:9

The Psalmist knew that with and through hope, we can find happiness in this life. Even though the principle of hope is a spiritual one, extending into eternity, it can also sustain us through the everyday challenges of life. We can, through hope, bring the strength of heaven into our homes, our workplaces, our minds, and our hearts. Our hope in God's promises empowers us with an eternal perspective.

December 16

O God, I am guilty of transgressions that make me ashamed, and I fear you'll leave me. Yet have you ever refused to forgive those who ask? Why would I be different? Reassured, I accept forgiveness and will share it with those who need it from me.

December 17

We are such stubborn folk, gentle God, only moving toward you when it's time for a baby, of all things! What an illogical story, yet you knew it would take something unexpected to get our attention. Be with us as we edge toward the manger again this year, both from curiosity and habit, pausing to kneel there because we are finally getting the message.

December 18

Bless all newborns, Lord, with hunger of soul and mind to match a growing, thriving body. At awesome moments like these, we, your "big children," feel your blessing wrapped around us like a baby's blanket. Give us wisdom, patience, humor, stamina, humility, joy, and grace to pass on to the children in our lives.

December 19

Depart from evil, and do good; seek peace, and pursue it.

—Psalm 34:14

Give me the tools for building peace, O God, when tempers flare—inside and outside these four walls. In your wisdom I daily try to impart, needed tools include a kind of heart and faith that measures each tiny rebuilt bridge a triumph.

December 20

O God, instill in my children the heart of an adventurer
off to explore every corner of your marvelous creation and
to find their place in it. Thank you for blessing the quest
and relieving my anxiety by promising to be a part of their
journey step by step.

December 21

I weave a silence on my lips,
I weave a silence into my mind,
I weave a silence within my heart.
I close my ears to distractions,
I close my eyes to attentions,
I close my heart to temptations.
Calm me O Lord as you stilled the storm,
Still me O Lord, keep me from harm.
Let all the tumult within me cease,
Enfold me Lord in your peace.

—Celtic Traditional

December 22

"Thou shalt love the Lord thy God with all thy heart, and with all thy soul, and with all thy mind. This is the first and great commandment. And the second is like unto it, Thou shalt love thy neighbour as thyself."

—Matthew 22:37–39

If I'm loving others the way I'm loving myself, we're all in trouble. May God awaken me to my life so I can help those I meet be awake to theirs. May God awaken all of us to a great, all-encompassing love for him.

December 23

Rest in the Lord, and wait patiently for him.

—Psalm 37:7

Those who wait patiently for God's direction find inner peace.
Godly patience brings peace with others.

December 24

And the Word was made flesh, and dwelt among us, (and we beheld his glory, the glory as of the only begotten of the Father,) full of grace and truth.

—John 1:14

Son of God, who came to Earth,
thank you for your love for us.
Son of Man, who dwelt among us,
thank you for your love for us.
Savior, who redeemed the world,
thank you for your love for us.
Jesus, living Word of God,
thank you for your love for us.

December 25

And the angel said unto them, Fear not: for,
behold, I bring you good tidings of great joy,
which shall be to all people. For unto you is
born this day in the city of David a Saviour,
which is Christ the Lord.

—Luke 2:10–11

Lord Jesus, today we celebrate your birth into our world.
We delight in your presence in our world. And I welcome
you again into my heart. With joy and love, I greet you.

December 26

The days after Christmas can sometimes be a bit of a let-down, but they can be peaceful, too. After all the preparation and rush, we have a little time to reflect and talk. Things that weren't "important" enough to get brought up at the big family meals make their way into conversation. Let me be grateful, Lord, for these gentle times of relaxation and renewal as we prepare for the end of the year.

December 27

Beloved, let us love one another: for love is of God; and every one that loveth is born of God, and knoweth God. He that loveth not knoweth not God; for God is love. In this was manifested the love of God toward us, because that God sent his only begotten Son into the world, that we might live through him.

— 1 John 4:7–9

God's love supports us so we can support others in love. In what ways is God supporting me today? In what ways, God, would you like me to support others?

December 28

Sometimes we feel alone. But when I reflect back on this year, I can see how even when I felt alone, I was not. With his presence, his Word, and his people, God comforts us. Father, thank you for those times I was aware of your presence, those times a scripture verse spoke to me, those times a person said just the right thing.

December 29

God of beasts and critters, bless them, for they bless me even when they shed on the couch and don't come when called. They love without strings and share the simplest joys of walks and catnaps, slowing me down to a pace you recommend.

December 30

I ask you to cleanse my heart today of all lingering resentments. I say I forgive something, but sometimes I have a hard time letting it go—I want someone to see my side and tell me I was right! But I want to walk free into the new year. Please let me let go of any bitterness or anger I am holding onto, so that I can keep my hands open to receive your mercy and grace.

December 31

We're closing out the year tonight! Dear Lord, I ask for safety for my family and my friends and all those we love, both tonight as people attend celebrations and drive home, and in the year to come. I ask that I have a clear eye in the coming year to see all the ways in which you bless me abundantly. And I thank you for your love that surrounds me, enfolds me, and heals me. With you at my side, I am never alone.